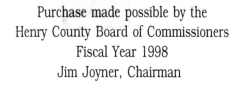

Always a
Reckoning

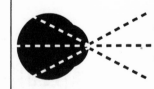

This Large Print Book carries the Seal of Approval of N.A.V.H.

Always a Reckoning

and Other Poems

Jimmy Carter

Illustrated by
Sarah Elizabeth Chuldenko

G.K. Hall & Co.
Thorndike, Maine

Published in 1995 by arrangement with Times Books, a
division of Random House, Inc.

G.K. Hall Large Print Core Collection.

The text of this Large Print edition is unabridged.
Other aspects of the book may vary from the original edition.

Set in 16 pt. News Plantin by Warren Doersam.

Printed in the United States on permanent paper.

Library of Congress Cataloging in Publication Data

Carter, Jimmy, 1924–
    Always a reckoning, and other poems / Jimmy Carter ;
illustrated by Sarah Elizabeth Chuldenko.
      p.   cm.
    ISBN 0-7838-1301-5 (lg. print : hc)
    1. Large type books. I. Title.
    [PS3553.A78144A79 1995b]
    811'.54—dc20   95-13851

Dedication

To my father, Earl, who labored all his life but also loved the good times, his innate goodness curbed by the Southern mores he observed, a man who relished discipline, who reached out to his son with love, always tempered with restraint;

to my mother, Lillian, who never would let racial segregation, loss of loved ones, ravages of age, or any other principalities or powers stop her sharing what she had or was with the least of those she knew;

to Rosalynn, who, most of all, has stretched my mind and heart and let me know what patience, love, and sharing mean;

to Rachel Clark, whose dignity and grace were heightened by a world in which, although apartheid reigned, she even managed to excel; and to others of her race and mine who suffer now from prejudice and, back then, were forced by law and threats to tolerate their plight in silence;

to people living in and near the town of Plains, who, all my life, have given me a microcosmic although true awareness of the greater world;

to those with whom I traveled on and under seas, with special thanks to Hyman Rickover, who goaded us to reach for higher dreams and duties than the mediocre ones we were inclined to tolerate;

to the few who seek to share their faith through words and simple deeds and sometimes bring a better life to those who rarely know *agape* love; and to those others, still in need, who'll never know religious acts like these;

to punishment or remorse for those who claim to speak for God, but only in his role as judge; for human rights oppressors in our own and other lands; for those who cause, condone, or disregard the suffering of the poor and weak;

to those many people, still with us or gone, not listed here in any special way, who've helped to mold my life, my thoughts and attitudes, and, unknowingly, to shape these poems;

to poets who write at times with simple beauty I can comprehend, including Dylan Thomas, whose work can touch me in a special way;

to Jim Whitehead, who came to Plains and helped me live with what I know;

to Miller Williams, who, with patience and his own particular examples, tried to teach me how a poem should mean;

to Sarah, just sixteen, who read the poems and sketched what each one meant to her;

and to the readers of this book, who, I hope, will draw from them some pleasure, stimulating thoughts, or memories to make up for my lack of erudition, skill, or artistry.

Contents

People

Places

Politics

Private Lives

People

Rachel

My young life, shaped by those I loved,
felt the gentle touch of Rachel Clark,
our neighbor on the farm, whose
    husband, Jack,
cared for the barn and did the kind of
    work
that we boys most admired. He tended
    mules,
and rang the cast-iron bell that brought
    an end
to sleep, and later tolled the time to
    rest.
His wife was small and quiet. Her brown
    skin
fixed her in our segregated world,
yet Rachel had the aura of a queen
that somehow wouldn't let the white
    folks ask
for her to do the chores around their
    place —
like cooking, ironing clothes or tending
    babes.
But she would volunteer with quiet grace
any time she learned the need was real.

15

For miles around, the farming folks
    would know
what Rachel did while working in the
    field.
I'd pick a hundred fifty pounds or so
of cotton if I never stopped to rest —
no man could do much more — but
    Rachel Clark
could pick near twice as much as second
    best.
At sundown we would tie what we had
    got
in burlap sheets, and watch the foreman
    weigh,
see for ourselves that Rachel had the
    most,
and if she topped her own best mark
    that day.
She'd put a lot more peanuts on the
    stacks,
hoe more weeds, shuck more corn —
    no one,
in fact, could equal anything she did.
These kinds of deeds that may seem
    small to some
were big events for us, in which we all
competed, as our farm life would allow.
When work was done, or when a heavy
    rain
made the fields too wet to hoe or plow

and open cotton bolls too damp to pick
sometimes she'd smile at me and mention
　　fish.
Then she and I would leave the farm
　　and walk
six miles or so to reach a stream she
　　knew.
These journeys gave us ample time to
　　talk —
or rather, I would listen to her
　　words,
as she would think a while, and then
　　hold forth
about God's holy way: how, when we
　　deal
with Nature, we are stewards of the
　　earth,
she'd say that blessings bring on debts to
　　pay,
describe the duties of a man and wife,
and say the brave and strongest need not
　　fight.
She'd tell how praying gave her life a lift,
and how it made her act and not just
　　talk —
like staying up all night with someone
　　sick.
It wasn't empty preaching, like in church:
sometimes I wasn't glad to reach the
　　creek.

Our bait was crawfish, lizards, crickets,
  worms,
or whatever she would recommend
for perch, catfish, and bass — which we
  called trout,
misnamed by our European kin,
or mine at least; I knew that Rachel's
  folks
were brought, themselves, to be my
  people's slaves.
The swamps and woodlands came alive
  for me.
She taught the way that every person
  craves
to learn. Our creels were empty flour
  sacks
that kept our catch in water, fresh and
  safe
from watersnakes and snapping turtles,
  that
would have left us bones instead of fish.
Rachel used exactly seven poles,
for reasons I could never figure out.
I asked her, "Why not eight or six?" She
  only
smiled at me, then went ahead and
  caught,
with luck or skill, five fish to one of
  mine.

She made it seem a favor, heading home
if some of hers would wind up in my
  sack.
Those might have been the best days I
  have known.

With my folks gone, I'd stay with her
  and Jack.
Newspapered walls all leaned, the sagging
  doors
stayed open, letting flies and breezes in.
I smelled the lye that cleaned the holy
  floors.
Saving kerosene, we slept at dusk
on lumpy cornshucks, not my feather
  bed.
They always made me feel like I
  belonged,
and knew what things were better left
  unsaid.
Although the food was plain and seldom
  changed,
I never thought our big house down the
  road
was better. They all knew I liked to be
with Rachel Clark. I guess my feelings
  showed.

In later years, I'd visit Rachel's home
in public housing; sometimes I'd find

her on the village street. Then, still a
    queen,
her apron sagging with a can of beer,
she'd laugh about what good times there
    had been,
and tell me what she thought I ought
    to do
in Washington, where I was working
    then.

Mister Woodruff and Old Bess

Life was hard in those Depression years.
Money was scarce, and swaps the way
we had to trade. Mister Woodruff,
at his stable, used to say
that no one got the best of him.

He heard a poor man had to sell
a mule, and bought her way below
the price he knew the animal
would bring in town. Unselfish now,
he said, "She's mine, but you feel free
to work Old Bess a few more days.
This weekend bring her in to me."
With thanks, the farmer kept the mule.

But Saturday, with miles to ride
to Woodruff's barn to close the deal,
the mule fell down, kicked twice, and
   died.
The farmer had to walk to town.

When he approached, the idlers stopped

their checker games. They all had heard
how bad the man had been outswapped.
They found it strange to see him there
with just a bridle, in distress.
Mister Woodruff walked up then
and said, "Well, Mister, where's Old
    Bess?"
The farmer told him what took place;
then, edging over toward the door
he blurted out, "I'll swear t' God,
your mule ain't never done that before!"

The County Boss
Explains How It Is

I'm here just to oblige, you understand.

I get an awful lot of criticism
serving all these folks who call on
   me
to meet their needs: some roadway
   paved, their son
or brother with a job, a welfare check,
a sheriff who don't notice when they
   buy
a can of Sunday beer or something
   stronger
in a jar.
            The poorest always want
more help and aren't too proud to pay
   me back.
I never ask much in return: a part
of what they get each month, and a hand
at polling time.

           Politics is hard.
They know I can't afford a big campaign!

It's natural if they want to give
    support
to me and a few mutual friends — the
    judge,
sheriff, and voting clerks. (It's bread on
    the water.)
The governor and state officials thank
a county that will always go their way.
That's how the people get the roads
    and jobs.

Sometimes you have to do a little
    prodding —
barns or shelters have been known to
    burn.
(I'm always off in Dothan at the time.)

So how can I be sure about the
    folks?
They don't mind our watching when
    they vote
or having ballots ready-marked.
                            It's them
that cash the checks, and see the
    pavement poured,
and drink the booze.
                Hell, if the law's not
    broken,
only bent a little, what's the harm
if all we do is seek a better life?

Some radicals would like to bring us
   down
and take charge here by generating strife.

I guess there's demagogues in every town.

A Motorcycling Sister

Her lives were always, simply said, her
   own,
So no one ever knew which one we'd
   come
To find — a charming southern lady who
Was dressed for tea, or one who made
   her home

A pad for biker gangs, Daytona bound,
Who'd stop and sometimes stay a week,
   as though
They'd found a mother — one who rode
   with them
On many trips. Once, down in Mexico,

She broke her leg, which kept her home
   awhile
But gave her extra time to freeze and can
Her garden's harvest for the crowds that
   came,
And ate, and slept on floors, then rode
   again.

Her final illness filled our town with men,

Leather-jacketed, with beards, who stayed
In shifts, uneasy, in her darkened room.
Telegrams were sent. The hearse was led

To graveside by those friends, two by
    two,
With one ahead: in all by thirty-seven
Large and noisy bikes. And on her tomb
They had inscribed SHE RIDES IN HARLEY
    HEAVEN.

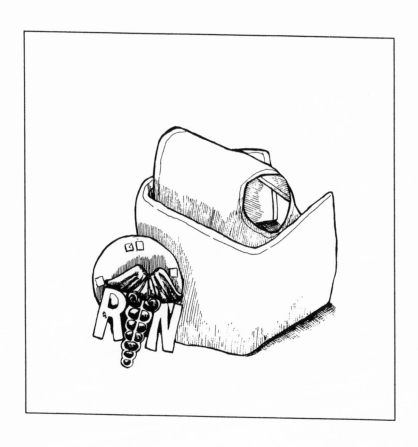

Miss Lillian

She would nurse
and when they couldn't pay
she would still be there.

She loved to laugh
and often laughed alone,
but didn't seem to care.

When she wept
not many tears would fall.
She never had learned how.

She died
and left us all behind.
What will we do now?

Miss Lillian
Sees Leprosy for
the First Time

When I nursed in a clinic near Bombay,
a small girl, shielding all her leprous
    sores,
crept inside the door. I moved away,
but then the doctor called, "You take
    this case!"
First I found a mask, and put it on,
quickly gave the child a shot and then,
not well, I slipped away to be alone
and scrubbed my entire body red and
    raw.

I faced her treatment every week with
    dread
and loathing — of the chore, not the
    child.
As time passed, I was less afraid,
and managed not to turn my face away.
Her spirit bloomed as sores began to
    fade.

She'd raise her anxious, searching eyes to
  mine
to show she trusted me. We'd smile and
  say
a few Marathi words, then reach and hold
each other's hands. And then love grew
  between
us, so that, later, when I kissed her lips
I didn't feel unclean.

The More Things Change

In a musty attic box I found
letters of my family in the War —
from places like Bull Run and
    Gettysburg
and places seldom mentioned in the
    books.

They said Jeb Stuart had praised some
    of them,
who served a cause and often gave their
    lives
not knowing how to tell the history
they made, except a private's point of
    view
set down in a simple line or two:

"We have about a half enough to eat,
green beef and flour, but very little
    salt.
Our company left Savannah heading
    north,
there was a hundred twenty-five of us,

but since then many of my friends have
  died
so now they's only thirty-six to fight.
I tell you, Mother, I am well
but am not satisfied."

A Committee of Scholars Describe the Future Without Me

Some shy professors, forced to write
about a time that's bound to come
when my earthly life is done
described my ultimate demise
in lovely euphemistic words
invoking pleasant visions of
burial rites, with undertakers,
friends, kinfolks, and pious pastors
gathered round my flowery casket
eyes uplifted
breaking new semantic ground
by not just saying
I have passed on
joined my maker
or gone to the Promised Land
but stating the lamented fact
in the best and gentlest terms
that I, now dead, have recently
　　　　　reduced my level of participation.

To One, Now Gone, Who Always Let His Hunting Partner Claim a Downed Bird

I never knew he did not see
that sharing his own needs or pain
would be a showing of his trust,
not putting burdens off on us.
Nourished by his selflessness
we leaned on him too much and now
inexplicably have lost
what I thought we'd always have.
We never knew adversity,
except our own, to seam his face.
And now with every glimpse of human
  grace
he comes to mind, not welcome yet,
not with the ever-escorting grief.
There has to be a special place for him,
who held in more than he could bear
to shield the rest of us from care.
A rarity
who showed us what *agape* means.

The Ballad of Tom Gordy

In '41 the Japanese
   took our troops on Guam,
Alive or dead — we didn't know.
   One was my Uncle Tom.

He was the Navy boxing champ,
   my hero with his crown.
Now with him gone, his family moved
   down to our Georgia town.

My grandma and my aunts felt Tom
   was not his wife's but theirs.
She could feel the coolness but
   stayed on to join their prayers.

What bound them all together was
   the hope and faith and dread.
When two years passed, the dispatch
   came:
my Uncle Tom was dead.

His wife and kids moved back out West

to start their lives again,
And after Tom was gone three years
  she wed a family friend.

The end of war brought startling news:
  Tom Gordy was alive.
Four years he had been digging coal
deep in a mountainside.

The women took the feeble Tom
  and smothered him with care.
He never would tell anyone
  what happened over there.

Tom Gordy soon regained some strength
  and craved a normal life,
But mother and sisters told him lies
  about his absent wife

Betraying him. Tom wanted her,
  but couldn't figure how
To bring her back or overcome
  her second marriage vow.

He got four years' back pay and made
  Commander, U.S.N.
It didn't take him long to find
  a woman's love again.

Tom closed the past except when his

three children came to stay;
When I would mention his first wife
he'd always turn away.

Once my submarine tied up
where she lived with her kin.
I went to visit them, afraid
they wouldn't let me in.

But all the folks they knew were called
when I first gave my name;
All night we danced and sang because
at least Tom's nephew came.

The Pasture Gate

This empty house three miles from town
was where I lived. Here I was back,
and found most homes around were gone.
The folks who stayed here now were
 black,
like Johnny and A. D., my friends.

As boys we worked in Daddy's fields,
hunted rabbits, squirrels, and quail,
caught and cooked catfish and eels,
searched the land for arrowheads,
tried to fly the smallest kite,
steered barrel hoops with strands of wire,
and wrestled hard. At times we'd fight,
without a thought who might be boss,
who was smartest or the best;
the leader for a few brief hours
was who had won the last contest.

But then — we were fourteen or so —
as we approached the pasture gate,
they went to open it, and then
stood back. This made me hesitate,
sure it must have been a joke,

53

a tripwire, maybe, they had planned.
I reckon they had to obey
their parents' prompting. Or command.

We only saw it vaguely then,
but we were transformed at that place.
A silent line was drawn between
friend and friend, race and race.

Places

Plains

Pioneering white men fought to claim
The land of Indians they sent West to
    die.
Our families moved in then to occupy
The rolling plains that gave the town its
    name.
There were only half a thousand souls,
White and black, the master and the
    slave.
Neither side forgot, nor ever gave
Each other ways to reach their common
    goals.

But now, as equals, free to rise or fall
Together, we have learned we must
    depend
On one another. Though the town is
    small,
We cherish it as haven, home, and friend,
And won't let strife or mischance bring
    to all
our dreams — our modest, tempered
    dreams — an end.

Of Possum and Fatback

I'd spend all night on possum hunts
with our neighbors, who were well-
respected men, but poor — the ones
who wouldn't waste a shotgun shell,
but shared their food and meager pay
with a mess of hounds, who'd lie and sun
and fight out in the yard all day,
too lazy for a rabbit run.
The dogs had equal family rights,
and came alive late afternoons,
to hunt and howl all through the nights,
feeding time for possums and coons.

The other hunters were grown men
but still they always wanted me
to go along, to be there when
someone had to climb the tree.
We'd take an ax, some bags, a coil
of rope, some lanterns, and flashlights.
(High-priced batteries and oil
were only used on blackest nights.)
We'd argue as we moved along
about the voices of our hounds:
knowing each distinctive song,

the melodies and quavering sounds.
"Old Bell's lost, just hear the bitch,"
"Hampton's back," "That's Blue Boy's
   wail."
And then would come the rising pitch
that said the dogs had struck a trail.

The owner got the choice of game
if his dog had struck it first,
so all of us would try to name
the lead dog as we crashed and cursed
through bramble, gully, swamp, and
   creek,
over fences, stumps, and logs.
Then we'd find the possum's tree
already half-climbed by our dogs,
straining as they leaped and whined,
all competing for the prize.

On lucky nights, our beams would find
two mirrors in the quarry's eyes.
We either had to cut the tree
to get the coon or possum down,
or climb up there and shake it free.
And when we had it on the ground
we'd have to keep the dogs at bay
and try to get it in a sack
before it died or ran away.

Each man hoped to take one back

to put in his own kitchen pot.
The dog race was a real contest,
since that was how good meals were got.
The top hound's family ate the best.
Fatback was the usual fare,
boiled for taste or fried for grease,
so wild game brought a welcome change
with cornpone, collard greens, and peas.

We liked the yarn about a man
out on a limb, an acrobat,
screaming down a fierce command,
"Shoot him, it's a damn bobcat!"
The reply came from the ground,
"Pa, we'll hit you with the gun!"
The man wailed, with an oath or two,
"Just shoot up here amongst us, son!
It's better'n what I'm going through."

Jokes and moonshine somehow let
the ones who didn't get their meat
believe they liked the cold and wet,
and just fatback to eat.

Peanuts

To me, a miracle: the blossoms send
A peg to penetrate the earth, to swell,
To make a seed, a hundred to the vine.

From five years old till I was almost
    grown
I dug and boiled them. Every day I'd
    walk
With twenty bags or so, three miles to
    town,
Sell all of them, then plod back home
    again.

Almost ignored, an omnipresent boy,
I learned how merchants cheat, which
    married men
Laid half-a-dollar whores, not always
    white;
The same ones touting racial purity
And Klansmen's sheeted bravery at night.

Up and down the single street, I'd stop
And try to sell, mostly wasting time
In busy places like the blacksmith shop,

Or in the quiet corner pharmacy,
Where waiting patients in the wire-
    backed chairs
Would hardly ever buy a thing from me.
The cobbler would take two bags at a
    time,
Without a word; I never had to make
A pitch to him, just pocketed the dime.

I'd watch the solemn sale of gasoline;
Five gallons at the most was pumped by
    hand
Up to a glass container, clearly seen
By everyone, confirmed, then down to fill
T-Model tanks. No man took on faith
What cost him sixteen hours in the field.
The men threw dimes at floorboard
    cracks to tell
Who'd buy a round of dopes (not yet
    called Cokes)
I hoped would wash down what I'd
    come to sell.

And at the livery stable, one old man
Would always interrupt his checker game
To heckle me. He'd miss the brass
    spittoon
To spray right at my feet, and then he'd
    try
To make me sing a song or dance a jig;

I never would, nor cut my price — but I
Would sometimes feed the mules or
   sweep the floors
To make a sale.

                I loved to deal with drummers
Toting cases of their goods to stores.
I think they saw me as a kindred soul
And bought from me the way they
   hoped to sell.

Long before I was ten years old
I learned to judge the whole community,
My standards just as good as those of
   preachers
Or scholars, who would teach philosophy
Or write their books.

                I knew the good folks were
The ones who bought their boiled
   peanuts from me.

The Day No One Came to the Peanut Picker

I remember when the field hands struck.
Everybody seemed to know,
although the paper never wrote it up
and few then had a radio.
Folks from all around came by to see
the idle picker with no crew
with the weather dry and right for work
and the peanuts ready, too.

I never thought they had a chance to win
with pay the same as all the other
workers in the field that year: for men,
fully grown and strong, a dollar,
which would buy a pair of overalls.
I heard a lot of people say
that, by God, they would never get as much
as two bits more a working day.

I didn't see how they could win at all.

The landlord only got one cent
a pound for peanuts or his fattened hogs,
and never charged a dime of rent
to workers in his houses, free to cut
all the firewood they could burn
and also with a family garden plot.
Some earlier, they might have won,
with peanuts fully ripe and likely lost
if not plowed up, and shook, and stacked,
but now they could wait longer in the
    sun.
The owner went to every shack
and gave, as he thought any Christian
    should,
the locked-in men a choice: to pay
all that they owed him, pack their
    household goods
before sundown, and move away,
or, come first light, be in the field again.
I never doubted they would stay.
A buck a day wasn't bad pay for then.

Itinerant Songsters
Visit Our Village

When some poets came to Plains one
  night,
two with guitars, their poems taught
us how to look and maybe laugh
at what we were and felt and thought.

After that, I rushed to write
in fumbling lines why we should care
about a distant starving child.
I asked how we can love the fear
and death of war, rejecting peace
as weakness; how a poet can dare
to bring forth out of memory
the troubling visions buried there,
and why we barely comprehend
what happens out in space.
                    I found
my words would seldom flow, and then
I turned to closer simpler themes:
a pony, Mama as a nurse,
the sight of geese, the songs of whales,
a pasture gate, a racist curse,

a possum hunt, a battle prayer.
I learned from poetry that art
is best derived from artless things,
that mysteries might be explored
and understood from that which springs
most freely from my mind and heart.

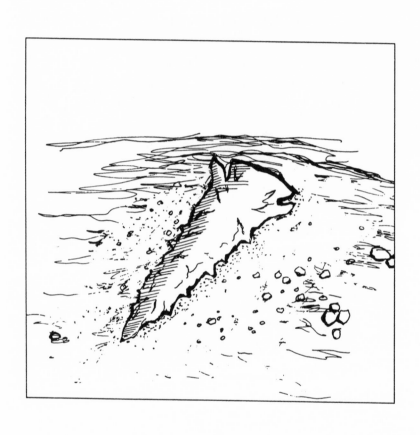

The History of a Point

Walking through a fallow field,
I found an arrowhead
more lovely than I'd ever seen,
up on an earthen pedestal
not packed by rain
but sheltered by the point itself.

Caressing it, I let my mind race back to
  when
a chief's son wore it as a charm,
but somehow lost it and then feared
calamities would come;

or when, nowhere near this place,
a hunter made a shot, close up,
sure his matchless arrow would not miss,
but then the deer escaped,
later to reach here, and to die;

or when, in war, it struck a brave
who pushed it through to save his life
but never saw it, hidden in his blood;

or perhaps this arrowhead

had such a beauty it was buried
with the artist who had shaped it.
Or none of these.

Without a trace of wood or bone
the point seems always to have lain alone.

A Reflection of Beauty in Washington

I recall one winter night
going to the White House roof
to study the Orion nebulae,
but we could barely see the stars,
their images so paled by city lights.

Suddenly we heard a sound
primeval in its tone and rhythm
coming from the northern sky.
We turned to watch in silence
long wavering *V*'s,
breasts transformed to brilliance
by the lights we would have dimmed.
The geese passed overhead,
and then without a word
we went down to a peaceful sleep,
marveling at what we'd seen and heard.

Flying into Japan and Seeing Mount Fuji Above the Clouds

We've climbed some peaks
that dwarf this flawless cone
seeming to float above Japan,
the whitest clouds turned drab
against its lustrous side.
Its calm,
its solitude and strength
all say
some things will abide,
if not
the fruitless, transient labors
of our lives.

a haiku

Fuji humbles us —
its strength and lasting beauty —
our own fleeting lives.

Priorities of Some Mexican Children

A sign was leaning toward adobe shacks
back from the road, across a dry plateau.
LLANOS it read, the same as our Plains.
When we stopped to photograph the view
three black-haired children hurried down
  a path
shouting something, eager to be heard.
"Get out your pocketbooks," I said,
"I can guess the word."
When they got closer, we could tell
it was not *dinero* but
lápiz and *papel*.

---

lápiz = pencil; *papel* = paper

Politics

My First Try for Votes

Uneasy in my first campaign,
I feared the likely ridicule,
but got up nerve and neared
some loafers I saw shooting pool.

I caught the eye of an older man
who seemed to know who I might be.
When I went up to him to speak
he cocked a bleary eye at me.

"Now, wait, don't tell me who you are,"
he shouted out. I stood in dread.
Bystanders paused. I blabbed my name.
He frowned. "Naw, that ain't it," he said.

Progress Does Not Always Come Easy

As a legislator in my state
I drew up my first law to say
that citizens could never vote again
after they had passed away.

My fellow members faced the troubling
  issue
bravely, locked in hard debate
on whether, after someone's death had
  come,
three years should be adequate

to let the family, recollecting him,
determine how a loved one may
have cast a vote if he had only lived
to see the later voting day.

My own neighbors warned me I had gone
too far in changing what we'd always
  done.
I lost the next campaign, and failed to
  carry
a single precinct with a cemetery.

A President Expresses Concern on a Visit to Westminster Abbey

Poet's Corner had no epitaph
to mark the Welshman's
sullen art or craft
because, they said,
his morals were below
the standards there.
I mentioned the ways of Poe
and Byron,
and the censored Joyce's works;
at least the newsmen listened,
noted my remarks,
and his wife, Caitlin, wrote.
We launched a clumsy, weak campaign,
the bishops met
and listened to the lilting lines again.
Later, some Welshmen brought to me
a copy of the stone
that honors now the beauty he set free
from a godhead of his own.

A Battle Prayer

All those at war
Pray to obtain
God's blessing.
It's with those in pain.

It Can Fool the Sun

Some people never say, "Let's go home,"
not having one, except a plastic sheet;
when cold, they try to find a warm air
   grate;
an empty doorway's better than the street,
and two share one refrigerator crate.

A shack that decent folks would ridicule
is where some others live, and don't
   complain.
They look up through the roof, smile
   and sigh,
"It can fool the sun, but not the rain!"

Hollow Eyes, Bellies, Hearts

We chosen people, rich and blessed,
rarely come to ask ourselves
if we should share our voice or power,
or a portion of our wealth.

We deal with problems of our own,
and claim we have no prejudice
against the people, different, strange
whose images we would dismiss:

Hollow eyes in tiny faces,
hollow bellies, gaunt limbs, there
so far away. Why grieve here
for such vague, remote despair?

Human debris tries to reach
a friendly port, however far.
We can't pay them mind forever,
wretched dregs from an ugly war.

With apartheid's constant shame
Black miners slave for gems and gold.
The wealth and freedom are not theirs;

White masters always keep control.
Bulldozed houses, olive trees axed;
terrorist bombs, funeral wails;
no courts or trials, prison still.
The land is holy, hate prevails.

One alone in a Chinese square
confronted tanks, while others fled.
He stood for freedom for us all,
but few care now if he's jailed or dead.

Visits in the dark of night
by lawful thugs — indrawn breaths
of fear, and then the last farewells.
The death squads won't admit the deaths.

Torture, murder . . . bitter loss
of liberty and life. But they
are friendly tyrants! What would all
our cautious questioning convey?

Why think of slaves, nameless deaths?
Best be still, as in other days.
Response was bland to Hitler's deeds —
Should we condemn our fathers' ways?

We chosen few are truly blessed.
It's clear God does not want us pained
by those who suffer far away.
Are we to doubt what He ordained?

With Words We Learn to Hate

We take lives in times of peace
for crimes we won't forgive,
claiming some have forfeited
the right to live.
We justify our nation's wars
each time with words to prove we kill
in a moral cause.
We've cursed the names of those we
      fought —
the "Japs" instead of Japanese,
German Nazis or the "Huns,"
and "Wops" — when they were enemies.

Later, they became our friends,
but habits live in memories.
So now, when others disagree
we hate again, and with our might,
war by war, name by dirty name,
prove we're right.

Why We Get Cheaper Tires from Liberia

The miles of rubber trees bend from the
  sea.
Each of the million acres cost a dime
nearly two Liberian lives ago.
Sweat, too,
has poured like sap from trees, almost
  free,
from men coerced to work by poverty
and leaders who had sold the people's
  fields.

The plantation kiln's pink bricks
made the homes of overseeing whites
a corporation's pride.
Walls of the same polite bricks divide
the workers' tiny stalls
like cells in honeycombs;
no windows breach the walls,
no pipes or wires bring drink or light
to natives who can never claim
this place as theirs
by digging in the ground.

No churches can be built,
no privy holes or even graves
dug in the rolling hills
for those milking Firestone's trees, who
  die
from mamba and mosquito bites.

I asked the owners why.
The cost of land, they said, was high.

Private Lives

Rosalynn

She'd smile, and birds would feel that
    they no longer
had to sing, or it may be I failed
to hear their song.

Within a crowd, I'd hope her glance
    might be
for me, but knew that she was shy, and
    wished
to be alone.

I'd pay to sit behind her, blind to
    what
was on the screen, and watch the image
    flicker
upon her hair.

I'd glow when her diminished voice
    would clear
my muddled thoughts, like lightning
    flashing in
a gloomy sky.

The nothing in my soul with her aloof

was changed to foolish fullness when she
    came
to be with me.

With shyness gone and hair caressed
    with gray,
her smile still makes the birds forget to
    sing
and me to hear their song.

Some Things I Love

Your enchantment in a lonely wood,
The fight and color of a rainbow trout,
My in-basket empty and a good new
  book,
Binoculars fixed on a strange new bird,
Sadie's point, and a covey of quail,
The end of a six-mile run in the rain,
Blue slope, soft snow, fast run, no fall,
A dovetail joint without a gap,
Grandchildren coming in our front door,
The same ones leaving in a day or two,
And life, till what rhymes best with
  breath
takes me from all things I share with you.

Difficult Times

I try to understand.
I've seen you draw away
and show the pain.
It's hard to know what I can say
to turn things right again,
to have the coolness melt,
to share once more
the warmth we've felt.

Always a Reckoning

There always seemed to be a need
for reckoning in early days.
What came in equaled what went out
like oscillating ocean waves.
On the farm, our wages matched
the work we did in woods and fields,
how many acres plowed and hoed,
how much syrup was distilled,
how many pounds of cotton picked,
how much cordwood cut and stacked.
All things had to balance out.

I had a pony then that lacked
a way to work and pay her way,
except that every year or two
Lady had a colt we sold,
but still for less than what was due
to buy the fodder, hay, and corn
she ate at times she couldn't be
on pasture.

       Neither feed nor colts
meant all that much that I could see,
but still there was a thing about

a creature staying on our place
that none of us could eat or plow,
did not give eggs, or even chase
a fox or rabbit, that was sure
to rile my father.

            We all knew
that Lady's giving me a ride
paid some on her debt, in lieu
of other ways — but there would be
some times I didn't get around
to riding in my off-work hours.
And I was sure, when Daddy frowned
at some mistake I might've made, he
would be asking when he could,
"How long since you rode Lady?"

Prosperity Doesn't Suit Everyone

One year when our cotton crop was good
and watermelons hit the market high
a circuit-riding tailor came to town.
My father felt the time had come to buy

a proper suit of clothes. He was measured
with flourishes. It came by mail.
  Impressed,
we could only stroke the striped serge,
still boxed. But when Sunday came at last

so did our kin, to see the grand display.
The pants and coat engulfed him like a
  child.
He wouldn't talk or go to church that
  day,
and no one in our family blinked or
  smiled.

I Wanted to Share
My Father's World

This is a pain I mostly hide,
but ties of blood, or seed, endure,
and even now I feel inside
the hunger for his outstretched hand,
a man's embrace to take me in,
the need for just a word of praise.

I despised the discipline
he used to shape what I should be,
not owning up that he might feel
his own pain when he punished me.

I didn't show my need to him,
since his response to an appeal
would not have meant as much to me,
or been as real.

From those rare times when we did cross
the bridge between us, the pure joy
survives.

I never put aside

the past resentments of the boy
until, with my own sons, I shared
his final hours, and came to see
what he'd become, or always was —
the father who will never cease to be
alive in me.

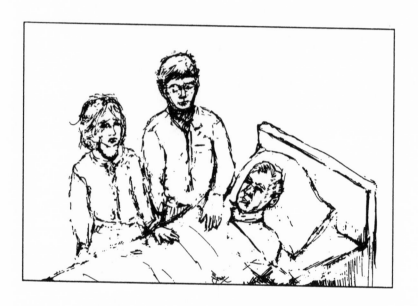

Of My Father's Cancer, and His Dreams

With those who love him near his bed
seldom speaking any more,
he lies too weak to raise his head
but dreams from time to time.
In one, he says, he sees his wife,
so proud in her white uniform,
with other nurses, trooping by,
their girlish voices aimed to charm
the young men lounging there.
Then her eyes meet his and hold.
A country courtship has begun.
They've been together thirty years.

Now, she watches over him
as she tries to hide her tears.
All his children are at home
but wonder what they ought to say
or do, either when he is awake
or when he seems to fade away.
They can't always be on guard
and sometimes, if his mind is clear,
he can grasp a whispered phrase

never meant for him to hear:
"He just seems weaker all the time."
"I don't know what else to cook.
He can't keep down anything."
He hears the knocking on the door,
voices of his friends, who bring
a special cake or fresh-killed quail.
They mumble out some words of love,
try to learn how he might feel,
then go back to spread the word:
"They say he may have faded some."

He'll soon give in to the rising pain
and crave the needle that will numb
his knowledge of a passing world,
and bring the consummating sleep
he knows will come.

A Winter Morning

My father's touch would end my childish
    dream,
fitful as it was. This venture off with him
introduced the grownup world to me.

I snuggled near him, cold wind in my
    face
until our pickup reached the proper place.
While it was still too dark for us to see

we heard the killdeer and a lone bobwhite
as birdsongs prophesied the end of night.
It was as near to heaven as could be.

We waited, anxious, till the brightening
    sky
showed other hunters at their stands
    nearby.
Guns began to fire, and doves to die.

Sport

Yesterday I killed him. I had known
for months I could not let him live. I
 might
have paid someone to end it, but I knew
that after fifteen years of sharing life
the bullet ending his must be my own.

Alone, I dug the grave, grieving, knowing
that until the last he trusted me.
I placed him as he'd been some years ago
when, lost, he stayed in place until I
 came
and found him shaking, belly on the
 ground,
his legs too sapped of strength to hold
 him up,
but nose and eyes still holding on the
 point.
I knelt beside him then to stroke his
 head —
as I had done so much the last few days.

He couldn't feel the tears and sweat that
 fell

with shovelfuls of earth. And then a
   cross —
a cross, I guess, so when I pass that way
I'll breathe his name,
and think of him alive,
and somehow not remember yesterday.

When We Lit the Kerosene Lamps

There seemed to be a feeling in the house
that something was there in the corners
in the dark corners
just beyond the light
like a warm and friendly vapor
coming back from days before —
Grandpa, maybe, or one of the hands
who used to work for us.

White boss or black servant
it wasn't very clear.

Light Comes
in Turkey Country

I know the forest on my farm
best at breaking day
when birdcalls seem to draw
the darkness back
that cages me.
The dim tree limbs
fragment the barely luminescent sky,
a metronomic whippoorwill
wakes the distant, lonely doves,
strangely wary when they call,
the ground and saplings come in view,
the pileated's crazy cry
is punctuated by its hammer blows on
    wood
and a barred owl wants to know
who cooks for me.
Distance takes the jagged edges off
the crows' more raucous sound
and then perhaps, perhaps,
a far-off gobbler's piercing call
ends all that reverie.
I move that way, very carefully.
I hardly breathe, and move that way.

Trout

Those who fish for trout
go where beauty is,
where air is incense, where
no poison stains.
Congenial friends may share
these lonely streams,
but they must stay past bend
or waterfall.
Testing oneself is best
when done alone.

We try to learn the secrets
of the stream,
how currents run, what drifts
in quiet depths
or sweeps around the stones
to tempt a fish;
what artifice can stir
the same desire
with feathers and some fur,
a barb within.
A trout is never trusting.

We learn by using

simple, ancient gear,
the history of an art —
and we learn patience, too,
sometimes the hardest part.

The solitude,
relief from care,
frustrating doubt
about our angling skills —
these stay with those who fish for trout.

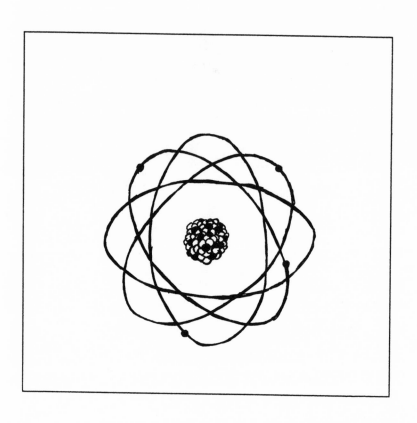

A Contemplation of What Has Been Created, and Why

I tried to fathom nature's laws
from twirling models and schoolroom
  sketches
of molecules and parts of atoms,
and nearly believed — but then came
  quarks,
bosons, leptons, anti-particles,
opposite turning mirror images,
some that perforate the earth,
never swerving from their certain paths.
I've listened to conflicting views
about the grand and lesser worlds:
a big bang where it all began;
of curved, ever-expanding space;
perhaps tremendous whirling yo-yos
that will someday reach the end
of cosmic gravity and then
fly back to where they can restart
or cataclysmically blow apart —
and then, and then the next event.
And will it be an accident?

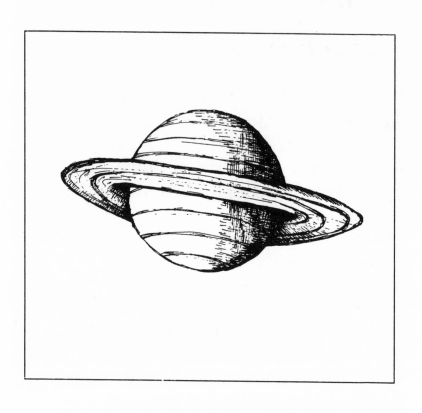

Considering the Void

When I behold the charm
of evening skies, their lulling endurance;
the patterns of stars with names
of bears and dogs, a swan, a virgin;
other planets that the *Voyager* showed
were like and so unlike our own,
with all their diverse moons,
bright discs, weird rings, and cratered
   faces;
comets with their streaming tails
bent by pressure from our sun;
the skyscape of the Milky Way
holding in its shimmering disc
an infinity of suns
(or say a thousand billion);
knowing there are holes of darkness
gulping mass and even light,
knowing that this galaxy of ours
is one of multitudes
in what we call the heavens,
it troubles me. It troubles me.

On Using Words

I first heard jumbled sounds
before they framed my infant thoughts
and didn't know beliefs and dreams
would ride on random consonants
and vowels in the air.

Now when I seek efficient words
to say what I believe is true
or have a dream I want to share
the vagueness is still there.

Life on a
Killer Submarine

I had a warm, sequestered feeling
deep beneath the sea,
moving silently, assessing
what we could hear from far away
because we ran so quietly ourselves,
walking always in our stocking feet.
We'd listen to the wild sea sounds,
the scratch of shrimp, the bowhead's
    moan,
the tantalizing songs of humpback whales.
We strained to hear all other things,
letting ocean lenses bring to us
the steady, throbbing beat of screws,
the murmurs of most distant ships,
or submarines that might be hunting us.
One time we heard, with perfect clarity,
a vessel's pulse four hundred miles away
and remembered that, in spite of every-
    thing
we did to keep our sounds suppressed,
the gradient sea could focus, too, our
    muffled noise,

could let the other listeners know
where their torpedoes might be aimed.
We wanted them to understand
that we could always hear them first
and, knowing, be inclined to share
our love of solitude, our fear
that one move, threatening or wrong,
could cost the peace we yearned to keep,
and kill our hopes that they were
   thrilled, like us,
to hear the same whale's song.

Index of Titles

Index of First Lines

About the Author

Jimmy Carter's first book of poems, *Always a Reckoning*, allows us to share his insights on such diverse experiences as his childhood on a South Georgia farm and his years as President of the United States. He is the founder and chairman of the Carter Presidential Center in Atlanta, Georgia.

Other books by Jimmy Carter include *Keeping Faith*, *Everything to Gain* (written with his wife, Rosalynn), and *Talking Peace*. He is also the proud grandfather of the illustrator of this book.

About the Illustrator

Sarah Elizabeth Chuldenko, an award-winning artist, is a senior at the San Francisco School of Fine Arts. After her graduation in 1996, she plans to enter the School of the Museum of Fine Arts in Boston, Massachusetts.

The employees of G.K. HALL hope you have enjoyed this Large Print book. All our Large Print titles are designed for easy reading, and all our books are made to last. Other G.K. Hall Large Print books are available at your library, through selected bookstores, or directly from us. For more information about current and upcoming titles, please call or mail your name and address to:

G.K. HALL
PO Box 159
Thorndike, Maine 04986
800/223-6121
207/948-2962